Portal
By
Browncherub

Myrah Duckworth
(B.Ed Hons)

BookLeaf Publishing

India | USA | UK

Presentation by *BookLeaf Publishing*

Web: www.bookleafpub.com

E-mail: info@bookleafpub.com

ISBN: 9789357619240

First edition 2023

*This book is dedicated to all those who are
willing to fight for their offspring every single
day of their lives.*

ACKNOWLEDGEMENT

I would like to thank everyone who has helped me raise my three brown cherubs and supported me through my good times and bad times. My family and friends. You know who you are.

Thank you to DeObia Oparei for reminding me to break the glass ceiling and get my creative juices flowing again.
Thank you to City Academy for seeing me and investing in my talent.
Thank you to my dear friend Sabina for helping me to actively explore my creativity.
Thank you to my Spiritual Psychologist, Toni Anne for giving me permission to be my 100% authentic self.
Thank you to my bestie Antoninette, for always, always being there for me and my family, no matter what, for all of my adult life.
Thank you to my husband Mark and my parents for supporting all of my ideas and for loving all that I am.
Thank you to my five babies for choosing me to be their Momma. I made some mistakes along the way, but I tried my best and I will always love you.

PREFACE

This book is an exploration of my amazing journey into and through motherhood. It is written to acknowledge all who have invested their blood, sweat and tears: life, love and laughter into their beloved offspring. The physical battles, the mental battles, the financial battles, the emotional battles and the spiritual battles that we fight each and every day to be the best mother we can be for each of our little ones. From the day we find out we are pregnant until the day we take our last breaths we love them with all that we are. And maybe even beyond that. There are, of course, exceptions to every rule and circumstance, but that is their story to tell. This is my story and I share it now, with you all.

Momma Bear

Momma Bear sits on the top level
Of my personality.
The part of me that defends
In my multi-layered energy.

The part of me that protects and shields
My three children from harm.
The part of me that growls loudly
And refuses to remain calm.

Leo sits in the middle level
Of my personality.
The part of me that attacks
In my multi-layered energy.

The part of me that fights
And goes bare-knuckle, toe to toe.
The part of me that roars fiercely
No matter friend or foe.

Zen sits at the base level
Of my personality.
The part of me that's stable
In my multi-layered energy.

The part of me that's rational
When there is chaos all around.
The part of me that 'Ommmms' softly
And quiets all of the sound.

A totem pole of all three
Exists within me.
Constantly, struggling, emotionally
Like Babba Vass, from my favorite Netflix
series... 'See'.

S.P.E.C.I.A.L.

S... Special
P... Place in my heart.
E... Everyday
C... Children
I... I will
A... Always
L... Love you.

Miracle Baby (Song)

Verse 1

Having a baby couldn't happen for me.
Or so I was told.
I was getting too old.
But each night I prayed for a baby.

Chorus:
There is no place too deep. I can reach you.
There is no place too dark. I can see you.
There is no place too far. I can find you.
There is no place too loud. I can hear you.
Wherever you choose to be.
I'll be there if you need me.

Because you are my miracle baby.
Yes, you are my miracle baby.

Verse 2

Your journey to me took so long.
So I celebrate you.
I see all you go through.
So each night I pray for you, baby.

Chorus:

Verse 3

You struggle and strain
And endure so much pain.
Yet you smile through it all.
Because you heard my call.
Each night I prayed for a baby.

Chorus:

Verse 4

You asked me why are you here?
I know the answer, my dear.
You answered my prayers for a baby.
So each tear cried by you, is a tear I cry too, because
you are my miracle baby.

Chorus

Kidney Bean

I wasn't aware that I was pregnant.
I didn't even know that you were there.
I wasn't feeling very well.
But I had an important event to attend.

My little Kidney Bean.

I went to the important event.
My stomach was cramping so bad.
But I put on a smile and got on with it.
After all, it was my event. I couldn't let my guests
down.

My little Kidney Bean.

The cramps were gradually getting worse.
So I went to the bathroom.
Sat on the toilet and hoped I would feel better
afterwards.
I wiped myself and there you were.

My little Kidney Bean.

I don't know how I knew, but I knew.
I don't know why you didn't just fall into the toilet.
It was like you wanted me to know you were there.
Like you wanted me to see you.

My little Kidney Bean.

I saw you. I acknowledged you.
With tears rolling down my cheeks.
My other hand covering my mouth.
To muffle the sound of my cry.

My little Kidney Bean.

You looked like a Kidney Bean.
But I knew you were a baby.
My baby.
Our baby.

My little Kidney Bean.

I didn't know what to do.
So I said a prayer for you.
I apologised to you.
I flushed you down the toilet.

My little Kidney Bean.

As the water swirled away.
I told you that I loved you.
I told you I would never forget you.
I thanked you for choosing me to be your Momma.

My little Kidney Bean.

I stood there for far longer than I should have.
One of my guests came to see if I was ok.

I smiled and said yes.
I went back and joined my important event.

My little Kidney Bean.

When I got home I told your Dad what had happened.
I told him that you looked like a little kidney bean.
He hugged me tightly and kissed my forehead.
We cried for you together.

My little Kidney Bean.

Three Countries (Song)

Chorus

My Father was born in Jamaica.
Both of his parents were born there too.
So he's a Yardie. A true Jamaican, through and
through.

My Mother was born in Barbados.
Both of her parents were born there too.
So she's a Bajie. A true Bajan, through and
through.

I was born in Birmingham, England.
Neither of my parents were born here.
So I'm a Brummie.
I'm not accepted as English
And certainly not British.

Three different countries
But none of them want me.
I don't fit in any place.
I don't know where I should be.

Verse 1

My ancestors were taken from Africa.
Beaten under the white man's whip.
Packed like nothing more than cattle.
On to the white man's ship.

Families separated.
Spread all over the world.
Kept as slaves. Worked to death.
No matter, big man or baby girl.

Chorus

Verse 2

I pray my children's children
And all of my descendants.
Will live in a place where they are free
And have full independence.

A place they feel accepted.
A place where they belong.
A place that embraces them.
So they don't have to sing this song.
A place where they are seen as equal.
A place where they can be brave and strong.
A place where they can fully thrive.
And live their whole lives long.

Chorus

Verse 3

So here I raise my family.
Continue our family tree.
I work hard to leave a legacy.
So they can be proud of me.

I want to help them do the healing.
From all the pain we are still feeling.
To use all the pain and sorrow.
To build a brighter tomorrow.

Chorus

Verse 4

Terrible things happened,
To us in History.
But the future is yet unwritten.
So let us tell our own story.

Maybe one day we will find a place.
Where the colour of our face,
Is not looked on in disgrace.
A home where we can all be proud of our race.

Chorus

Let's hope the time is not too far.
When we can truly celebrate who we are.

I Wore White

Today, I wore white.
A full white outfit.
White trousers.
White t-shirt.
Even white shoes.
I've never worn a full white outfit before.
Well maybe on my wedding day.
But that was different.
That was a special occasion.
Today, I wore white.
Just because it looks nice.

I didn't have to worry about getting dirty.
No grass stains from their trainers.
No chocolate fingerprints from their snacks.
No makeup marks from my daughters.
No paint, no play dough, no sand.
No glue, no glitter, no tomato ketchup.
Nothing to worry about at all.

But it made me sad.
Sad because I felt redundant.
Sad because I felt surplus to requirements.
Sad because I was no longer needed.
My children have grown up.
They no longer need me.

But then I smiled.
A very small smile.
Maybe one day.
Not any day soon.
But maybe, one day.
I won't be able to wear white again.
Because maybe one day.
I'll be a grand-momma.

Drumsticks (Song)

My son used to be so sad.
Now he's such a happy lad.
Since he got his drumming pad.
With his drumsticks. (x2)

When he needs something to hit.
He likes to go and sit.
All alone on his drum kit.
With his drumsticks. (x2)

He loves his weekly treat.
I love to watch him tap his feet.
As he plays the music beat.
With his drumsticks. (x2)

He likes to play football.
Sometimes he likes to fight a brawl.
I like to see him standing tall.
With his drumsticks. (x2)

Son, I believe in you.
I know your wishes will come true.
No matter what you do.
With your drumsticks. (x2)

No More (Song)

Chorus

How many more of our sons have to die?
How many more of our mothers have to cry?
No more, no more, no more
No more, no more, no more

I watched the horrific footage on the TV screen.
The scared child running through the street.
I clutched my chest and held my breath.
As my heart stopped, missing a beat.

I can't believe he got murdered
In the broad light of day.
I'm horrified. I fell to my knees.
And I started to pray.

Chorus

A parent should not have to bury their child.
Our youths shouldn't have to run scared or hide.
They say the pen is mightier than the sword.
So I'ma write down every word.

Flip my smile into a frown.
Stand up tall and straighten up my crown.
I'll hold on tight and write.
I won't fight, two wrongs don't make a right.

Chorus

Our boys aren't the enemies.
They are our sons, our babies.
This poor boy and so many others.
Our sons, our children, our brothers.

One day it could be my son.
It could be him, it could be anyone.
I won't march, I won't riot, I won't petition.
I will use my voice. I'm on a mission.

Chorus

The laws of this land weren't written for us.
But God nah sleep and so I trus.
That boy's life wasn't taken in vain.
God sees and knows our pain.

B. A. B. Y.

B... Be
A... Always
B... Beside
Y... You

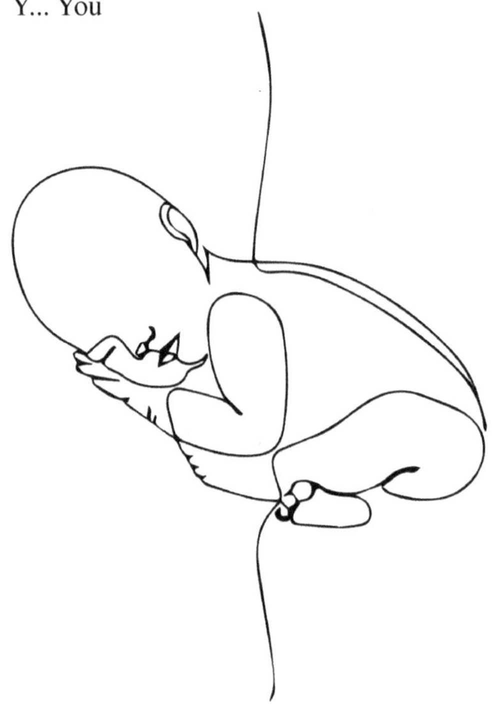

In Love With Me (Song)

Chorus
I love my wide hips.
I love my full lips.
I love my big grey afro.
I leave it, let it grow.

Verse 1

No photoshopped images influencing me.
About how I'm supposed to be.
How I'm supposed to look.
Isn't written in a book.
My unique designs are imprinted on my DNA.
So I give thanks everyday.
For everything I have,
To love and be loved.
I'm not absorbing any negative energy.
I'm not being judged.

Chorus

I'm in love with me.
Yes, I'm in love with me.
I don't care what you see.
I don't exist for you.
I exist for me.

Verse 2

I don't need fake nails
No extra lashes
Or cosmetic surgery.
I'm not working hard each day
To feed the cosmetic industry.

I rebel against the status quo
I do exactly what I choose.
I either win or I learn because for me
There is no loss.

Chorus

Verse 3

Don't you dare tell me what to do
Because I am a woman.
I'll do what I came to do.
I'll do everything I can.
Cellulite and stretch marks,
Grey hair and wrinkles, things could be worse.
I embrace these signs of aging,
They are a blessing, not a curse.

Chorus

Verse 4

Saggy tits and flabby bum.
My body's still a temple.
Go to the gym or eat the cake,
Life doesn't have to be a battle.

I love my wide hips.
I love my full lips.
I love my big grey afro.
I leave it, let it grow.

Saviour

I was weak because I never stood up for you.
I was weak because I should have made you my priority.
I was weak because I tried to forget you.
I was weak because I never even tried.

I apologise because I never gave you a chance.
I apologise because I thought you were a mistake.
I apologise because it wasn't your fault.
I apologise because I should have known better.

Please forgive me for being weak.
Please forgive me for being scared.
Please forgive me for being a hypocrite.
Please forgive me for not being worthy.

Thank you for choosing me to be your mom.
Thank you for teaching me about myself.
Thank you for helping me grow into the person I am today.
Thank you for offering me this valuable Karmic lesson.

You are my saviour because now...

I always try to be humble.
I always try to be nonjudgmental.
I always try to be compassionate.
I always try to be a better person.

I love you.

23

Thicker Than Water (Song)

Verse 1

Blood is thicker than water,
Might sound good to you.
But from where I'm standing,
That shit ain't true.

It's time to speak my truth,
Say what I see.
Talk about my friends and family.
Talk about how they've treated me.
Talk about my reality.

This song gonna make some people vex.
They gonna wanna hot up my phone with their text.
They gonna wanna say 'You can't say that!'
They gonna wanna tell me how
I'm supposed to chat.

Chorus

So I'ma tell dem haters.
Kiss my ass like they oughta
'cause for me, blood ain't thicker than water (x2)

Verse 2

Too many of them chat
Behind my back.
Now it's time to clap back
and write this track.

Chorus

So I'ma tell dem haters.
Kiss my ass like they oughta
'cause for me, blood ain't thicker than water (x2)

Verse 3

See my friends now
They've stood by my side.
Shoulder to shoulder
Through the turns of the tide.

Helping me out, through my times of struggle.
Helping me out, when I've had to juggle.
Helping me out, when I've been broke…had no
money.
Helping me out, not thinking it's funny!

Chorus

So I'ma tell dem haters.
Kiss my ass like they oughta
'cause for me, blood ain't thicker than water (x2)

Verse 4

To some of my family.
I have to raise my cap.
'cause to be quite honest
They ain't all crap.

Still it makes me feel uncomfortable.
When they're invited to sit around the family table.
Whilst me and mines are still left out.
That shit makes me want to scream and shout.

And the lies are spread.
And they be putting me down.
And they come back and tell me.
Now I'm wearing a frown.
And my heart is broken.
And my head is bowed.
So now it's time for me…
To SHOUT OUT LOUD!!!

Chorus

So I'ma tell dem haters.
Kiss my ass like they ought'a
'cause for me, blood just ain't thicker than water (x2)

So if you're the black sheep of your family.
Take a deep breath… (breath)
Repeat after me…

Ya'all can kiss my ass like ya oughta.
'cause for me, blood ain't thicker than water. (x2)

Yes..
Ya'all can kiss my ass like ya oughta
'cause for me blood ain't thicker than water (x2)

I said..
Ya'all can kiss my ass like ya oughta
'cause for me blood ain't thicker than water

Am I worried they ain't gonna like my flow?
Nahhhhh
That ship sailed long ago.

L.O.V.E.

L...Little
O...Ones.
V...Very
E...Emotional.

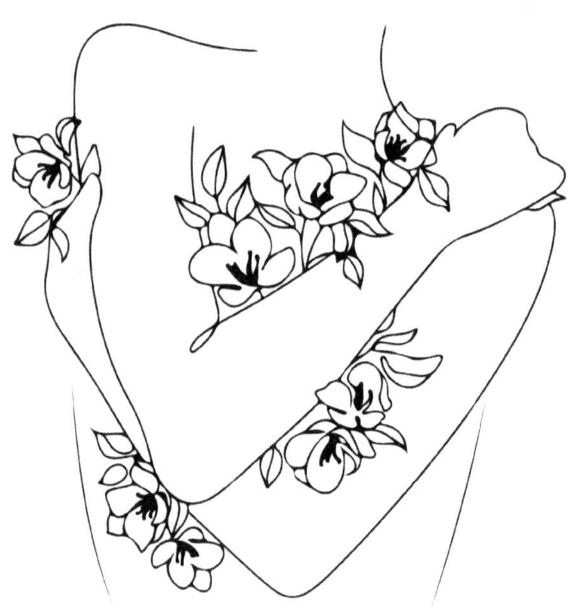

The One That Got Away (Song)

Verse 1

I used to go out every weekend.
Clubbing with my best friend.
Shaking my ass on the dance floor.
Wishing it would never end.

Having so much fun.
Music stops, lights turn on.
I'd still be there wanting more.
Dancing til it's just me one.

Verse 2

My friend be getting loads of attention.
Talking to all the guys.
I used to think I was invisible.
Until I lockcd on your eyes.

You brought me a drink or two.
You said I didn't have to pay.
At that time I never knew.
You'd be the one that got away.

Chorus

Away, away, away.
Away, away, away.

Away, away, away.
The one that got away.

Verse 3

You told me that you loved me.
You wanted me to be your girl.
I was too young for all of that.
I wanted to see the world.

You promised you would wait for me.
I believed all you had to say.
You said that I was free.
And then you just walked away.

Chorus

Verse 4

Our year together passed so quickly.
Talking on the phone.
I couldn't believe you just left me.
Left me all alone.

It's been years since I last saw you.
I still think of you everyday.
There's a place in my heart for you.
The one that got away.

Chorus

Verse 5

I wonder how life's been treating you.
I hope you're satisfied
I'm tempted to message you.
But I have never tried.

I wonder if you think of me.
Or reminisce about back a day.
I wonder if you consider me.
Your one that got away.

Away, away, away
Away, away, away
Away, away, away
You're the one that got away

Verse 6

I dream of how things might have been.
If we had stayed together.
But I'm so blessed to have the life I have now.
Roll the dice on that, I coulda never.

My handsome husband is wonderful.
My gorgeous children are amazing.
Our home is full of laughs and love.
The Lord I'm daily praising.

Verse 7

As we travel on life's journey.
We meet people along the way.

Some will stay and some will go.
That is needless to say.

But not everyone will be remembered
As the one that got away.
Away, away, away
Away, away, away
Away, away, away
The one that got away.

Autism Moms

Autism Moms are extra nice.
Lots of sugar, a touch of spice.
We bend and bow.
But never show.
How deeply our feelings really go.

To stop our children melting down.
As passersby just look and frown.
We live to serve and to protect.
And every speck we must detect.
And everywhere we must inspect.

They think we can't control our child.
They think we are so meek and mild.
They think we don't know what to do.
When everything's upsetting you.
But of course, we always knew.

Autism Moms love beyond measure.
Our children are our worldly treasures.
We'll cut the label from the vest.
We'll hold them tightly to our chest.
And yes...we always look forward to a rest.

Autism Moms are made of stardust.
So in us, our children place their trust.
Autism isn't bad or wrong.
We are here to comfort you our whole lives long.
It's just a different way to sing your heart song.

Alpha and Omega (Song)

Verse 1

Years and years we spent apart.
We went our separate ways.
I tried reaching out to you.
I missed you all those days.

Chorus

You aren't my one and only.
There were others in the past.
But you're my Alpha and Omega
I know our love will last.

Echo
Alpha x4
Omega x4
Alpha x4
Omega x4

Chorus

Verse 2
Not a single day passed by,
I didn't think of you.
I was so sad… so alone.
Didn't think I'd make it through.

Chorus

Verse 3
Twenty long years later.
You came back into my life.
Now we have a family.
I'm so proud to be your wife.

Chorus

Echo
Alpha x4
Omega x4
Alpha x4
Omega x4

Verse 4
I love you. I adore you.
You are my husband. My best friend.
I know we'll be together…
Until the very end.

Chorus

Echo
Alpha x4
Omega x4
Alpha x4
Omega x4

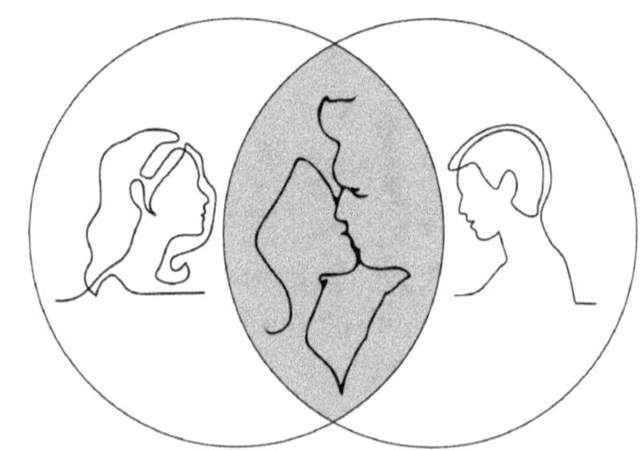

Frustration

Any form of discrimination.
Causes me so much frustration.
It makes me feel angry. It makes me feel sad.
It drives me crazy. It makes me so mad.

I have to make myself focus on my positivity.
And not get consumed by their negativity.
It's so easy to turn into that which I despise.
It's so easy to start to see the world through their
eyes.

It's so easy to hate, to judge and condemn.
It's so easy to start to think like them.
To wish them removed from the face of the planet.
To pick up a pen and start to plan it.

But I'm grateful it is my skin which is black.
Because once my soul turns that colour there's no
coming back.
So I stay in the light.
And I do what is right.

I take a deep breath and I sigh.
I remind myself that I have to try.
To remember who I am and why I am here.
And not be the one constantly living in fear.

I know you see me, and yes I see you.
For I know that which is real, and that which is true.
Unlike you, I can manage my frustration.
I do not let it become intimidation.

I do not let it become a hate-filled shout.
Or write it on a sign to keep others out.
I do not let it become an excuse to be mean.
I do not use it to prevent others from being seen.

But yes, I understand the feeling of frustration.
Living my life in an unfair nation.
But I am a part of the entire creation.
And that is why I believe in salvation.

Ts and Cs (Song)

Verse 1

A question somebody once came up and asked me.
Is your glass half full or half empty?
I stopped for a moment…hmmmm (pause)
I gave it some thought.
Trying to remember what I had been taught.

Then the Universe answered, "It's all 'bout the
glass."
Don't let it slip,
From your lip,
While you're taking a sip.

It might smash into pieces all over the floor.
And you'll be left wondering, what was it all for?
Sitting on your ass.
Surrounded by broken glass.
Just sitting on your ass.
Surrounded by broken glass.

Chorus

We spend our lives with such difficulties.
Instead of simply reading life's Ts and Cs.
We spend our lives trying to find some ease.
Instead of simply reading life's Ts and Cs.

Why do we suffer, struggle and strain?
Watching our money going down the drain. (Deep
voice)
If we followed the rules there would be less pain.
We would all see how much we could gain.

Chorus

Verse 2

What are these terms and conditions?
We don't seem to understand.
How to make things easy,
And take the upper hand.
Universal Laws and Hermetic Principle,
Understand this and life becomes simple.

Chorus

Verse 3

So let's break it down and see what we find.
Close our mouths and open up our minds.
Universal Law in no particular order.
This really can make your thinking broader.

The law of polarity.
The law of vibration.
The law of gender.
The law of attraction.

The law of action.

The law of relativity.
The law of compensation.
The law of perpetual transmutation of energy.

The law of rhythm.
The law of correspondence.
The law of cause and effect.
The law of oneness.

Chorus

Why spend your life with such difficulties?
Just simply read life's Ts and Cs.
Why not spend your life, living at ease?
Simply read life's Ts and Cs.

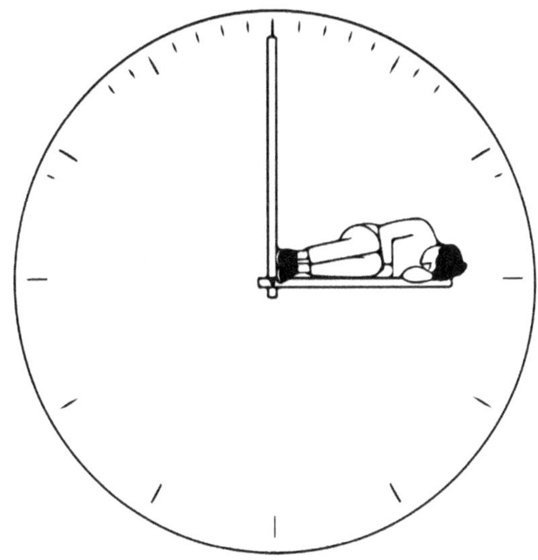

M.O.T.H.E.R.H.O.O.D.

M... My
O... Overwhelming
T... Thoughts.
H...Heartbeats
E...Eternally.
R...Rarely
H...Have
O...Others
O...Overstood such
D...Devotion.

All Kindsa Special (Song)

Verse 1

I knew your name.
Before you came.
Then you were placed in my arms.

You had such charms.
I vowed no harm,
Would ever come your way.

Chorus

So I have to say.
So I have to say.
I will protect you.
I will protect you
From everything.
Life may bring
Your way.

And that's because…
And that's because…
You're all kindsa special.
You're all kindsa special.

Verse 2

I felt no shame.

When you weren't the same.
As all of the others.

I never want another.
Because I'm your Mother.
So I'll love you every day.

Chorus

Verse 3

No room for blame.
My heart's aflame.
You make me so very proud.

So I will shout out loud.
Even in a crowd.
I'm there for you come what may.

Chorus

You have a special place in my heart.
You have a special place in my heart.

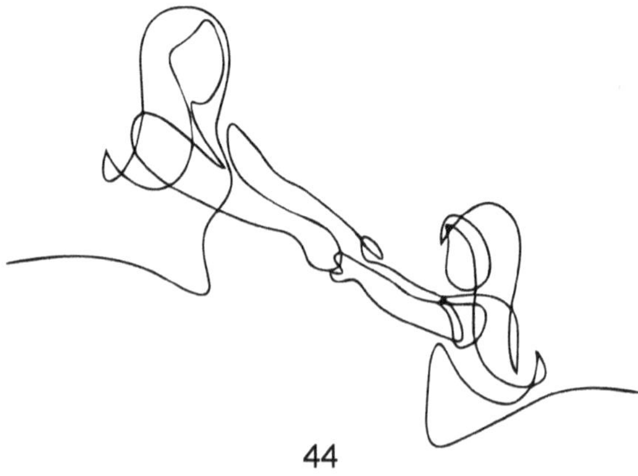

Graduation

I always wanted to graduate
From University.
I even left my home
And lived in a completely different city.

I studied hard
And eventually got my degree.
I hoped my family
Would be so proud of me.

I went on to teach
That was my plan all along.
I thought it would make me happy.
Wow, was I wrong.

What actually makes me happy
Is living a simple life.
Being a mother to three gorgeous humans
And being a loving man's wife.

So I graduated in life, you see.
Being a mother of three.
They have made me.
The person I always wanted to be.

The End